DISNEP PRESENTS A PIXAR FILM

THE INCREDIBLES

HOW TO USE THIS BOOK

Read the captions in the eight-page booklet and, using the labels beside each sticker, choose the image that best fits in the space available.

•

Don't forget that your stickers can be stuck down and peeled off again. If you are careful, you can use *The Incredibles* stickers more than once.

•

You can also use *The Incredibles* stickers to decorate your own books.

Written and edited by Lindsay Fernandes
Designed by Dan Bunyan

First American Edition, 2004
04 05 06 07 08 09 10 9 8 7 6 5 4 3 2 1

Published in the United States by
DK Publishing, Inc.
375 Hudson Street
New York, New York 10014

ISBN 0-7566-0588-1

Reproduced by Media Development and Printing Ltd, UK
Printed and bound by L-Rex, China

Dorling Kindersley would like to thank:
Lisa Gerstel from Disney and Krista Swager from Pixar for all their help with this book.

MR. INCREDIBLE

Heroic Mr. Incredible dedicated his life to fighting crime and saving lives, but after a spate of lawsuits all Supers were made to retire. For years he leads a "normal" life until a mysterious call lures him out of retirement.

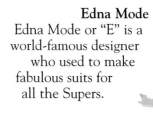

Heroic household
Mr. Incredible is married to a Super called Elastigirl. They have three children— Violet, Dash, and Jack-Jack.

The good old days
Bob's den is filled with mementoes from his crime-fighting days, including a key to the city.

A formidable fellow
Saving people from burning buildings, capturing bank robbers, and of course, rescuing cats from trees—it's all in a day's work for Mr. Incredible!

Back in action
Bored by civilian life, it doesn't take much to persuade Bob Parr to become Mr. Incredible once again!

Edna Mode
Edna Mode or "E" is a world-famous designer who used to make fabulous suits for all the Supers.

Bob Parr
Forced to hang up his Super suit for good, Mr. Incredible assumes the identity of Bob Parr and works for an insurance company called Insuricare.

Out of fashion!
E thinks Mr. Incredible's old blue suit is out of date and decides to make him a new "dramatic" one.

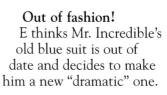

In training
Determined to get into top condition once again, Bob pumps iron at the local trainyard!

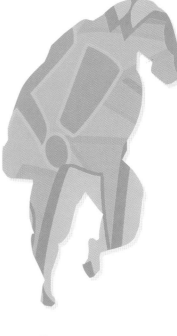

Strong man
Mr. Incredible can burst through walls with ease and lift cars as though they're as light as feathers, but no task is too small— he even helps little old ladies cross the street!

Outstanding outfit
Designed by E, Mr. Incredible's new suit has all the latest gadgets a Super could wish for. The secret homing device comes in very handy!

A cunning disguise
To conceal his identity, Mr. Incredible wears a mask over his eyes. Who wants the pressure of being "super" all the time?

Out of shape
Mr. Incredible puts on so much weight when in retirement, it takes him a few attempts to squeeze into the pod that will be air-dropped onto the island of Nomanisan.

To the rescue
Best friends, Mr. Incredible and Frozone, battle the out-of-control Omnidroid.

Teamwork
In the past Mr. Incredible worked alone but when he's captured by Syndrome he learns to accept help— and who better to come to his aid than his very own Incredible family?

Frozone
In retirement he's known as Lucius Best but really he's a Super called Frozone. He can create ice from the moisture in the air and used to be the coolest hero around!

ELASTIGIRL

In the golden age of heroes, Elastigirl used her amazing stretchy body to fight crime. Now she's happy living a normal life as Helen Parr. She is married to Mr. Incredible and is a devoted mother to their three children.

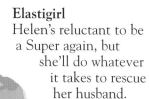

Stretching
Occasionally, Helen uses her powers at home—but only when the neighbors aren't watching!

Elastigirl
Helen's reluctant to be a Super again, but she'll do whatever it takes to rescue her husband.

A limber lady
Helen has the amazing ability to stretch like a piece of elastic and is as flexible as she was fifteen years ago!

Helen Parr
Helen adapts to civilian life quite well, but trying to lead a "normal" life with an extraordinary family isn't always easy!

Beware!
Bad guys have no chance against this high-kicking housewife!

Flexible fabric
Helen's suit has been designed by E with her special power in mind. It's made of elastic so it can stretch as far as she can!

Elastigirl in action
Inside Syndrome's compound Helen must be quick-thinking and agile to get past the guards.

THE INCREDIBLES

Incredible!

Violet's force field

The Parr Family

©Disney/Pixar

©Disney/Pixar

©Disney/Pixar

Mr. Incredible

Dash

©Disney/Pixar

Fighting the Omnidroid

©Disney/Pixar

Syndrome

©Disney/Pixar

©Disney/Pixar

Dash

At home

Velocipods

The Omnidroid

©Disney/Pixar

©Disney/Pixar

Shrinking Violet

©Disney/Pixar

Elastigirl

©Disney/Pixar

©Disney/Pixar

©Disney/Pixar

Good old days

THE INCREDIBLES

Syndrome

Bob Parr

Mr. Incredible

Jack-Jack

Edna Mode

Mr. Incredible and Frozone

Dash

Elastigirl

Violet

Edna

Elastigirl in action

Testing Jack-Jack's suit

Mirage

THE INCREDIBLES

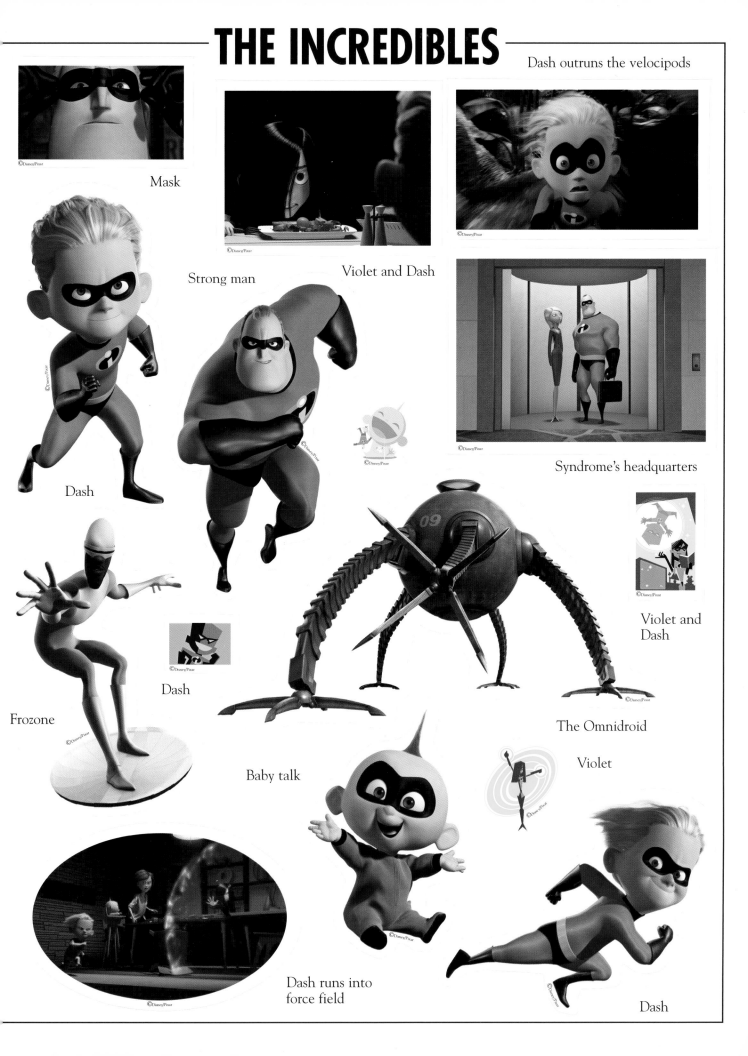

Dash outruns the velocipods

Mask

Violet and Dash

Strong man

Syndrome's headquarters

Dash

Dash

Violet and Dash

Frozone

The Omnidroid

Baby talk

Violet

Dash runs into force field

Dash

THE INCREDIBLES

Violet

Syndrome

Mr. Incredible
and Jack-Jack

Frozone

Jack-Jack
eating

Working
alone

Elastigirl

Jack-Jack

Limber
lady

In the drop
pod

High kicks

Bathtime for Jack-Jack

Jack-Jack

Outstanding
outfit

Training

JACK-JACK

Nearly two years old, Jack-Jack is the youngest member of the Incredible family, but unlike the others, he doesn't seem to have Super powers. It's not a problem though—he's still incredibly cute!

Baby talk
He can't talk yet so the only thing that comes out of his mouth is gibberish!

Fireproof romper suit
In her special testing lab, E checks that Jack-Jack's teeny-weeny Super suit is fireproof. It's machine washable too!

Family feuds
Jack-Jack likes nothing better than watching the chaos that's caused when his older brother and sister argue.

Messy meals
Jack-Jack does what babies do best—making an incredible mess at dinnertime!

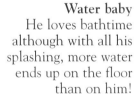

Water baby
He loves bathtime although with all his splashing, more water ends up on the floor than on him!

Jack-Jack
With his big blue eyes and innocent grin, Jack-Jack seems harmless to his babysitter. But there may be more to this tiny toddler than meets the eye...

Kidnapped
Bob and Helen are worried when Syndrome kidnaps Jack-Jack, but Jack-Jack surprises the villain who gets more than he bargains for!

VIOLET

As a shy and awkward teenage girl, Violet possesses the perfect Super power—she can disappear in seconds! She can also generate force fields which come in very useful when fighting bad guys and little brothers!

Schoolgirl crush
Violet thinks her brother Dash can be a little insect, especially when he teases her at the dinner table about her crush on Tony Rydinger!

A shrinking violet
Insecure and prone to blushing, Violet desperately wants to be just like everyone else.

Violet
At first Violet is not very confident using her powers, but she soon realizes she's a true Super. It's in her blood!

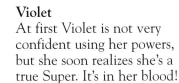

Invisible shield
Violet can surround herself in a special protective bubble. Once she's inside, no one can get to her—not even Syndrome's goon

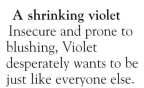

Silly squabbles
When Dash slaps Violet on the back of the head she throws an invisible force field in his path as he runs at high-speed—ouch!

Vanishing act
Violet's suit is made from a special material that disappears when she does!

DASH

With superhuman speed and a mischievous nature, Dash can easily get into trouble! But when he gets chased by Syndrome's guards, being super-fast helps him to escape!

Catch him if you can!
Getting hold of Dash when he's on the go can be tricky, but Helen manages to stop him with her stretchy arms.

Rapid little rascal
When you're lightning-fast creating havoc is easy. At school Dash puts thumbtacks on his teacher's stool during class, but he's so fast not even a video camera can catch him in action!

"The Dash"
Dash loves the excitement of being a hero. The family's adventure on Nomanisan was the best vacation ever!

Restless
Dash gets tired of being told to act "normal" by his parents and doesn't see why he should hide his powers. What's the point of having powers if you don't get to use them?

Cool costume
Dash's outfit is designed to withstand the heat that's generated when his legs and arms whirl around as he runs!

Super-fast
When he's running at full speed, Dash is even faster than the velocipods, Syndrome's super-turbo vehicles.

SYNDROME

Mr. Incredible's evil nemesis Syndrome tries to wreak havoc on the world just so he can pretend to save it and become the hero he's always longed to be. It's lucky the Incredibles are there to foil the villain's plans!

Buddy
He was once Mr. Incredible's biggest fan. He even wanted to be his sidekick "Incrediboy." But when his idea was rejected by his hero, Buddy turned into the bitter and revengeful Syndrome.

Omnidroid
Developed by Syndrome to be the ultimate weapon, this intelligent robot has the ability to *learn* how to fight its opponents!

An evil plan
Syndrome unleashes the Omnidroid on the city and tries to fight it himself, but things don't quite go according to plan!

Mean machine
After Mr. Incredible defeats the first Omnidroid, Syndrome plans to invite the hero back to face a bigger, "badder" version.

Syndrome's headquarters
On Mr. Incredible's return visit to the island of Nomanisan, Mirage picks him up using a high tech monorail system that transports them through the secret base.

Mirage
This mysterious woman tells Mr. Incredible that she works for the government, but really she's Syndrome's beautiful sidekick.